A GENTLEMAN PUBLISHER'S COMMONPLACE BOOK

'When, in 1812, *Childe Harold* was published,
Byron woke up to find himself famous
and his publisher, John Murray,
woke up a gentleman.'

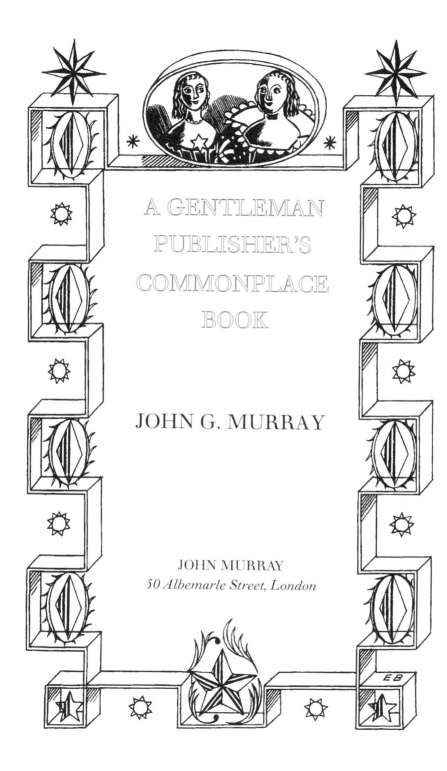

A GENTLEMAN PUBLISHER'S COMMONPLACE BOOK

JOHN G. MURRAY

JOHN MURRAY
50 Albemarle Street, London

Endpapers: John Piper
Title page: Edward Bawden design
for *The Lady of Bleeding Heart Yard*
by Laura Norsworthy
Contents page: Osbert Lancaster
from John Betjeman's *Continual Dew*
Dedication page: Dove by Reynolds Stone
Illustrations on half-titles of main sections:
Osbert Lancaster from *The Saracen's Head*
Frontispiece photo: Tim Mercer

This volume has been compiled,
designed, edited and typeset
by John R. Murray in admiration of his father

First published in 1996
by John Murray (Publishers) Ltd
50 Albemarle Street, London W1X 4BD

A catalogue record of this book is available
from the British Library
ISBN 0-7195-5623-6

Typeset in Monotype Walbaum 12pt
Printed and bound in Great Britain by
the University of Cambridge Press

FOR DIANA

whose wisdom, humour and support over more
than fifty years contributed so much

John Murray colophon
by Reynolds Stone

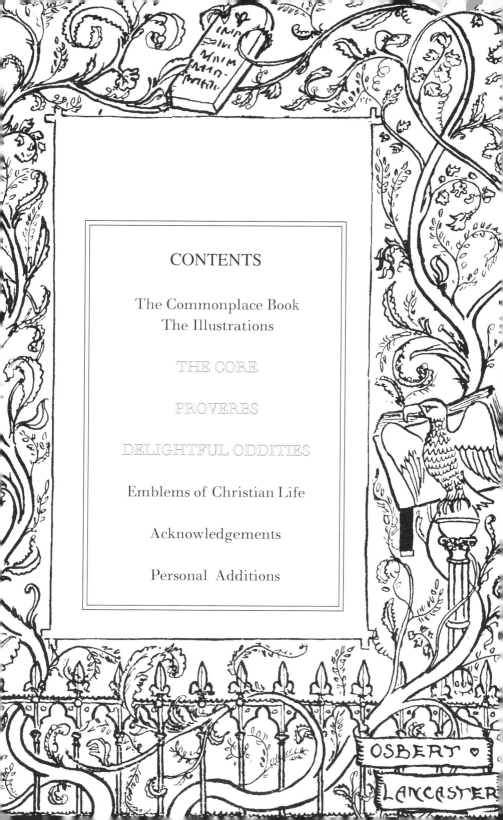

CONTENTS

OSBERT ♡

LANCASTER

'Maid of Athens 'ere we part,
Give, O give me back my heart,
For altho' it's yours tonight
Murray's have the copyright.'
Osbert Lancaster

The Commonplace Book

This slim volume has been gathered from my father Jock Murray's commonplace book which he kept throughout his life. Whenever he came across something wise, thoughtful, inspiring, witty or simply odd he would write it into a tiny blue notebook which he always kept in his inside jacket pocket.

He wrote usually in very fine pencil. But the longer he carried the notebook around with him the more the pencil faded, so that when he had finished it the early pages would, quite often, be indecipherable. Whenever possible he would copy out the items into his master commonplace book which, as the years passed by, became legendary. Unfortunately he did not always find time to do this, so when I went through it after his death I found that it contained only a fraction of what was scattered through more than forty small notebooks.

I decided to set myself the task of gathering together everything that remained legible. This was like reliving my father's life. The notebooks included quotations, proverbs, advice and jokes imbued with wisdom and humour, and provided, over sixty years, by his authors, friends and family who all used to feed him with additions.

Osbert Lancaster would descend on him most evenings
at 50 Albemarle Street, after completing his Pocket
Cartoon for the *Daily Express*, full of gossip and usually
with something new for the commonplace book. Freya
Stark would send contributions from Arabia, Axel
Munthe from Capri, and Peter Quennell would pass
down gems from the floor above while editing the
Cornhill Magazine. Kenneth Clark would arrive one day
with a Ruskin epigram and Margaret Lane with some
quip from the Brontë household. In addition to these, my
father picked up pithy proverbs and quotations as well as
words of profound wisdom from typescripts he read.
I think that the best usually came from those he reluc-
tantly turned down. Wherever he travelled he would be
seen pencilling some new find into his notebook.

Making a selection from everything I extracted from
the little blue notebooks has not been easy, but I have
tried to include something for every mood. As the true
pleasure of a commonplace book is the random nature
of its contents, no special order has been followed. The
intention is for you to 'surf' it and discover your own
favourites.

I have, however, made three divisions. The first, the
Core, is the main body of the book. I have extracted
the Proverbs as these meant so much to my father and
I felt that some of them would be lost if left in the Core.
It also seems to me that proverbs require a certain state
of mind which is best not combined with, say, a John
Piper riddle about a wheelbarrow and manure. I have
also included a category called Delightful Oddities as
this is exactly what they are. They always gave my

father particular pleasure and I can hear him chuckling over them, clicking his fingers in his characteristic manner.

Finally, and perhaps most important, my father was not always very accurate about attributions, and this has not been helped by the illegible state of some of the entries in his notebooks. So if you find howlers do please let me know so I can correct them. I have tried to verify as many as possible but have probably caught only a few.

The nature of a commonplace book is that it catches the *bon mot* which is often fleetingly heard in a speech or indistinctly overheard *en passant*. It is hard to keep in mind, until the little notebook has been extracted safely from the inside jacket pocket, and it is laid to rest, even if a little distorted, on the page.

I hope you will enjoy this small volume as much as I have enjoyed compiling it to celebrate a remarkable publisher.

The Illustrations

The illustrations and decorations are in themselves almost a commonplace book. Going through all the folders in my father's room at 50 Albemarle Street after his death was a veritable voyage of discovery. I felt as if I was prying into his life, but was sure he was enjoying watching me from above. These folders were full of decorations, illustrations and doodles that had been sent, or been given, to him by his friends and authors over a lifetime as a publisher.

3

There were contributions from John Piper (my brother's godfather), Osbert Lancaster (my sister's godfather), Freya Stark (my godmother), John Betjeman, Katharine Tozer, Kathleen Hale, Edward Bawden, Eric Ravilious, Edward Ardizzone, Beryl Cook and many others. Some were little sketches at the end of letters, some were fully worked-up watercolours. Reynolds Stone's wood engravings were accompanied by the wood blocks, and John Craxton, who produced such fine jacket designs for Paddy Leigh Fermor's books, sent a series of idiosyncratic Christmas cards featuring cats.

These folders revealed to me a publisher who was meticulous about detail and design. He was not only an editor who was totally dedicated to his authors' writings but also someone who cared passionately about the appearance of his books and who had an infallible eye for the lie of type on the page and for good design. He would, for example, commission Reynolds Stone to produce decorations for Freya Stark's books of essays, Eric Ravilious for a new design for the *Cornhill Magazine,* and as early as 1937 John Piper, Osbert Lancaster and others to create a truly unique design for *Continual Dew* by John Betjeman, which included double-page spreads on bible paper. Reynolds Stone also produced a new John Murray colophon.

In addition, authors and friends would send my parents cards or sketches to celebrate special occasions or to poke gentle fun at recent events – Orlando the Marmalade Cat portrayed with Grace acting out *Two Middle-aged Ladies in Andalusia,* Val Biro's view of the nuns of Stanbrook Abbey searching for their lost ring in their fishpond (inspired by a chance remark from my father who had just returned from visiting the nuns), Beryl Cook's touching painting of Archie shading Jumbo's eyes from her saucy pictures in *The Works*. In addition to drawings and doodles my father loved bellied rules and all kinds of printers' decorations and borders. He had a remarkable collection of printers' type sample books and books on typography. Finding complete sets of *Alphabet and Image* and *Signature* on his shelves showed that he was no dilettante but someone with true knowledge and feeling for type. Included in the following pages, therefore, are samples of borders, rules and other embellishments that he used over the years. In fact all the decorations were either used by him or designed for him at one time or another.

He always boasted that he learnt the art of typography from setting type in the nude with Robert Gibbings, who evidently had a strong belief that the best results were achieved if one was unhindered by clothes. As my father used to remark: 'It was alright for him as he was so hairy. It was somewhat different for me.'

John R. Murray

'You rang, Mr Murray?'
For John Murray's bicentenary dinner menu
1768 – 1968
Osbert Lancaster

THE CORE

Reynolds Stone wood engravings for various
books by Freya Stark

'There is no beauty that hath not some
strangeness in proportion.' Francis Bacon

'Happiness is no laughing matter.'
   Archbishop Richard Whateley of Dublin

'The causes of events are always more important
than the events themselves.' Cicero to Atticus

'After sitting next to Mr Gladstone I thought he was the
cleverest man in England. But after sitting next to
Mr Disraeli I thought I was the cleverest woman in
England.'
   Princess Marie Louise, Queen Victoria's granddaughter

'Some speakers electrify their listeners;
others only gas them.'

'I never read a book before reviewing it. It prejudices
a man so.' Sydney Smith

'It is a great error to suppose that people are rendered
stupid by remaining always in the same place.'
   William Cobbett

'A filthy mind is a perpetual feast.'
   From Osbert Lancaster

On the debate as to who wrote Shakespeare's sonnets:
'If they were not by Shakespeare, then they were
by someone of the same name.'

John Betjeman's suggestion for the jacket for
Penelope Betjeman's
Two Middle-aged Ladies in Andalusia

'People love to be nice but you must give
them the chance.' Auguste Renoir

'Confusion was immediately restored.'
   An expression used in the Second World War

'All beginnings are delightful, the threshold is
the place to pause.' Goethe

'The Pagets were like a family of Schopenhauerian
hedgehogs coming together for warmth – all their
prickles bristling.'
   Peter Gunn in *Vernon Lee*

On the flyleaf of an MS in a Syrian monastery, 6th
century AD: 'Who shall seek this book to read it
and shall not return it to its owners, may inherit the
halter of Judas for ever.'
   From Stewart Perowne

'Mieux vaut un petit amour qui chauffe qu'un grand qui
brûle.' On a plate seen in a Paris market

An old Scot when asked what was the difference
between the Free Presbyterian Church and the
Wee Free Church: 'There's nae so much difference
in this world but in the next: whereas we go straight
oop they go straight doon.'

'Her journalism, like a diamond, will sparkle more if it is
cut.' Raymond Mortimer on Susan Sontag

Field Marshal Sir William Robertson after the First
World War made a speech at a school prize-giving:
'Boys, I have a great deal to say to you but it won't take
long: so remember it. Speak the truth. Think of others.
Don't dawdle.'

'A slight touch of friendly malice and amusement
towards those we love keeps our affection for them,
I find, from becoming flat.'
   Logan Pearsall Smith, *Forgotten Years*

'I like reviewing books because it makes me
want to read them.' Overheard at a literary party

'A pink bon-bon stuffed with snow.' Debussy's
description of Grieg's music, quoted by Gerald
Moore in *Am I Too Loud?*

'I rather would entreat thy company
To see the wonders of the world abroad,
Than, living dully sluggardized at home,
Wear out thy youth with shapeless idleness.'
   Shakespeare, *The Two Gentlemen of Verona*

'Love us when we are dirty, for everyone will love us
when we're clean.' Gogol, quoted by Gordon Craig

'May God steel our hearts without hardening them.'
   Henry James

'Facts are not born free and equal.' C. V. Wedgwood

'In the field of observation, chance favours the
mind that is prepared.' Pasteur

'Cherish the past, adorn the present, create for
the future.'

'A young Apollo, golden-haired
Stands dreaming on the verge of strife,
Magnificently unprepared
For the long littleness of life.'
  Mrs Frances Cornford on Rupert Brooke

'The rich stuffing of her digressions almost kills the
flavour of the bird itself.' John Raymond on Rebecca
West's *Black Lamb and Grey Falcon*

'We become what we behold.' William Blake

'This world is a comedy to those who think, a tragedy
to those who feel.' Horace Walpole

On seeing two women shouting to each other across a
road from their doorsteps, Sydney Smith remarked to
his companion: 'A fine example of people arguing from
two different premises.'

'Max Beerbohm did not like a talker who did not
listen or a listener who did not talk.'
  New Yorker

'Life is a terminal disease.'

On reading *Two Middle-aged Ladies in Andalusia*
Kathleen Hale sent Jock this picture showing
Orlando and Grace following in
Penelope Betjeman's footsteps

'Don't marry money but go where money is.'
  Victorian dictum

'The main support of life is work — if it doesn't
let you down.'

'We are all in the gutter, but some of us are looking
at the stars.' Oscar Wilde

'It is the function of poetry to harmonize the sorrows
of the world.' A. E. Housman

Lady Winchelsea, when in 1903 her family had called
the doctor to her, sent down a message when he arrived
to say that she was too ill to see him.

'Short agreements make long friends.'
  Mrs Gaskell to her publisher

'The bridge of a sinking ship, one feels, is scarcely the
ideal place from which to deliver a lecture on the
technique of keeping afloat.'
  Kenneth Tynan, referring to Noël Coward's attack on
  young playwrights and their plays

'Adjectives are sirens; they betray all whom their
music beguiles. Enslave them and you are master
of the poetic art.' George Rylands

'I prefer Offenbach to Bach often.'
  Sir Thomas Beecham

'The ruthless self-absorption of old age'
  From Peter Green

'The flies that keep the oxen from ploughing'
  Chekhov on reviewers

'When Socrates spoke, the people said how inspiring,
but when Demosthenes spoke, the people said let
us march.'   Adlai Stevenson

'It is the function of literature to create, from the rough
material of actual existence, a new world that will be
more marvellous, more enduring and more true than
the world that common eyes look upon . . . '
  Oscar Wilde

'If she be not fair to me, what care I how fair she be.'
  Quoted by Elizabeth Barrett Browning

'A little wine spilt, a little oil stolen, these are the
prices of contentment.'

As an old Scots woman said when she was asked if she
would take some water with her whisky: 'I have troubles
enough without adding to them.'
  Quoted by Neville Lytton in a letter to Lady Lovelace

'Genius is an infinite capacity for giving pain.'

'Oh memory, thou fond deceiver.'
  Oliver Goldsmith, *The Captivity*

Ralph, Lord Lovelace's proposal letter to Margaret Stuart
Wortley: 'If you find yourself unwilling to accept me,
will you please pass this letter on to your sister Caroline.'
Both refused but he married the eldest sister Mary.
  Quoted by Lady Wentworth in her *Memoirs*

'Nothing so clarifies the moral sense as a drop of
aesthetic sensibility.'
  Edith Wharton about Bayard Cutting

'A piano without pedals'
  André Gide on the French language

'A tangled network of man-traps for conscience'
  Gladstone on Income Tax

' . . . that's why I avoid writers: 'tis a bad trade,
exhausting people of their better qualities, replacing
them by wicked vanities.'
  Vernon Lee in a letter to Maurice Baring

'Greatness consists of bringing all manner of
mischief upon mankind, and goodness in removing
it from them.'
  Henry Fielding

Oscar Wilde on Arthur Symons: 'An egoist without
an ego'

'Stealing from one source is plagiarism, while stealing
from many is research.'

Wood engraving for the *Cornhill Magazine*
by Eric Ravilious

Contraceptives: 'What Protestants use on all conceivable occasions'

'So coldly sweet, so deadly fair' Byron

Sir Edward Salisbury of Kew: 'Consistency is the foible of the feeble mind.'

'What more dost thou want when thou hast done a service? Art thou not content that thou hast done something comfortable to thy nature, and dost thou ask to be paid for it, just as if the eye demanded a recompense for seeing or the feet for walking?'
  Marcus Aurelius

'We are all actors who cannot become something before we have first pretended to be it.'
  W. H. Auden

'I believe in getting into hot water – it helps keep you clean.' G. K. Chesterton

'A psychologist once said that we know little about the conscience except that it is soluble in alcohol.'
  Thomas Blackburn in *London Magazine*

Rebecca West at the 1959 Foyle's Literary Lunch referring to booksellers: 'The most agreeable servants of civilization'

'Hold fast to that which is good.' A prayer

'The mania for phrases has dried up your heart.'
  Flaubert's mother to Flaubert

'You cannot legislate the heart, you can only contain it
on sufferance for a while.' E. Johnson

Flaubert could only write while stroking a ruler.

'Blood is thicker than water, and much nastier.'
  G. B. Stern

'A tiny core of stillness in the heart'
  D. H. Lawrence

'Father doesn't hear what Mother says,
and Mother hears what Father does not say.'

'Where others see but the dawn coming over the hill,
I see the sons of God shouting for joy.'
  William Blake

'A little is all very well, but too much is enough.'
  Richard Hughes

'Be kind to people on your way up because you will meet
them again on your way down.' Wilson Mizner

'Better a live sparrow than a stuffed eagle.'
  Edward FitzGerald

'He immatures with age.' Harold Wilson on Tony Benn

A view enjoyed for nearly fifty years, looking from
Hampstead Heath across to Highgate Church.
Edward Ardizzone for John Betjeman's *Ring of Bells*

'The greatest thing in the world is to know how to belong to ourselves.' Montaigne

'If you do not expect the unexpected you will never find it.'
   Heraclitus, quoted by Freya Stark

'Some of the staleness of our civilization is that we now have methods of decoding so much of it that it already seems overlong. When nothing is at the back how exciting is the future?'

'Here lies Martin Elginbrodde,
Have mercy on his soul, Lord God,
As I would do if I was God
And you were Martin Elginbrodde.'

'I am armed against love with a breastplate of reason.'

'I can work indefatigably at the corrections of a work before it leaves my hands, but when once I have looked on it as completed and have submitted it to the inspection of others, it becomes next to impossible to alter or amend.' Charlotte Brontë on *Shirley*

'Whom does one care to tease that one does not also care to kiss?'
   Robert Browning to Ian Blagden

'It takes a great deal of history to produce a little literature.' Henry James

'Advice is always dangerous, but good advice is fatal.'
  Oscar Wilde

'Reason cannot prevail where reason cannot penetrate.'
  From Peter Quennell

'Love is not looking in each other's eyes, but looking
together in the same direction.'
  Antoine de Saint-Exupéry

'Many live wires would be dead ones if it were not for
their connections.' *Evening Standard*

'Never blow your own trumpet: if you do that, other
people will be loth to do it for you.'
  Max Beerbohm's advice to a young reporter

'Some callers can stay longer in an hour than others
in a week.' From a calendar

'What is the conscience but a pair of breeches which
while it serves as a cloak both for lewdness and
nastiness, may be readily let down in the service
of either?'
  Jonathan Swift

'Shall I form your minds or cram you for a First?'
  An Eton master to his pupils

'Eggheads of the world unite, you have nothing to lose
but your yokes.' Adlai Stevenson

'I feel that one lies to oneself more than to anyone else.'
  Byron

'A man, sir, should keep his friendships in constant
repair.' Dr Johnson

'Creaking waggons last the longest.' Queen of Bohemia

A man seen searching for something under a street lamp
was asked: 'Are you sure you dropped it here?' 'Oh no, I
dropped it on the other side of the street, but there is
more light here.'

'I had become, with the approach of night, once more
aware of loneliness and time – those two companions
without whom no journey can yield us anything.'
  Lawrence Durrell, *Bitter Lemons*

'No cause so vile that some human being will not be
found to defend it'
  Norman Douglas, *Old Calabria*

'If I laugh at any mortal being,
'Tis that I may not weep.' Byron

'Only great men change their minds.'
  Adlai Stevenson

'I have heard of the milk of human kindness before, but
I never expected to meet the original cow.'
  A. J. Balfour

Freya Stark explaining to a relatively unsophisticated
audience the genius of Mr Norman Hartnell.

Osbert Lancaster

'The Earl of Portsmouth (*circa* 1800) would slaughter
his own cattle with an axe, shouting: "That serves them
right, the ambitious toads."' Tangye Lean

'Latent ambiguity' Legal expression

A GPO engineer to a lady complaining of a fault
on her telephone: 'Madam, your impulses are clearly
confused.'

'Life is short: let us love one another; there is nothing
else worth living for.'
  William Cory to Scott Holland from Eton

'Prune the luxuriant, the uncouth refine,
But show no mercy to the empty line.'
  Alexander Pope

'Poor Byron . . . he always kept his friends in hot water
during his life and it seems his remains will be of no
easy management after his death.'
  John Cam Hobhouse

'He has not learnt the lesson of life who does not every
day surmount a fear.' Emerson

'Only the insane take themselves seriously.'
  Max Beerbohm

'Culture is what is left when you have forgotten
everything.' M. Herriot

'Nothing in all the known world of politics is so
intractable as a band of zealots, conscious that they
are in a minority, yet armed by accident with the
powers of a majority.'
  Samuel Morley

'Forgiveness to the injured doth belong,
But they ne'er pardon, who have done the wrong.'
  Dryden, quoted by Byron

'Like all very selfish people she slipped easily into
the role of martyr.'
  Christopher Sykes on Lady William Russell

In a sermon given by a Congregational minister:
'If you have a spark of hope – water it.'

Byron to John Murray on whether the MS of *Childe
Harold* should be shown to potential reviewers: 'I will
have no traps for applause.'

'Just as an acorn grows into a great fir tree . . . '
  In a sermon given by a naval chaplain at Dartmouth

'Any intelligent fool can invent further complications,
but it takes a genius to attain, or recapture, simplicity.'
  E. F. Schumacher

'With whom can I retrace the laughing parts of life?'
  Byron to Dallas in 1811 on the death of three
  contemporaries

27

'Without contraries there is no progression.'
  William Blake

'Deserved praise is no more than the payment of
a debt, but flattery is a present.' Dr Johnson

'Cease, mortals, to conserve your prime
In vain attempts at killing time
For Time, alas, what e'er you do
Is sure to end in killing you.'
  Lines written by Palmerston to William
  Lamb's sister

'Scandal has something so piquant — it is a sort of
cayenne to the mind – that I confess I like it, particularly
if the objects are one's particular friends.'
  Byron, reported by Lady Blessington when deploring
  scandal in London against him

'Life would be dull without human error.'

'You can tell what God thinks of money when you look at
those to whom he has given it.'
  A man in a train to the publisher Colin Eccleshare

A Soviet joke:
Q. 'What's the difference between capitalism and
communism?'
A. 'Under capitalism, Man exploits Man. Under
communism it is exactly the opposite.'
  David Levy in *The Spectator*

Maudie Littlehampton bookshop-visiting
to promote John Murray's latest list.
Osbert Lancaster

'It is a terrible thing to part from people one has known a very short time.' Oscar Wilde

'The drumming silence of the country on the ears of the town dweller'

A hangover: 'A nutritionally self-induced type of cerebral malfunction.'
  Evening Standard on Prof. Marks' dietary research

'Being published by the Oxford University Press is rather like being married to a Duchess: the honour is almost greater than the pleasure.' G. M. Young

'Stanley Baldwin always hits the nail on the head, but it doesn't go in any further.'
  Critic of Stanley Baldwin's speeches

'The nonsense which was knocked out of them at school is all put back gently at Oxford and Cambridge.'

'A man always looks dead after his life has appeared.'
  Byron on biographies of living people

'There is no reciprocity. Men love women, women love children, children love hampsters.'
  Alice Thomas Ellis

'Men so little understand the comfort of talking a great deal about nothing at all.'
  Lady Granville to her sister in 1810

Lord Alfred Douglas on writing:
'To fight with form, to wrestle and to rage
Till at the last upon the conquered page
The shadows of created beauty fall.'

'One of the large French rivers – wide, placid, seemingly
endless, no current, occasional felicities on the bank,
shallow and *just* moving'
    A description of George Moore's later prose. Rupert
    Hart-Davis in a letter to George Lyttelton, 1957

'What is democracy? An aristocracy of blackguards.'
    Byron

'*Andiatorocte* is the title of a volume of poems by
the Rev. Clarence Walworth. It is a word borrowed
from the Indian and should, we think, be returned to
them as soon as possible.'
    From a review by Oscar Wilde in the *Pall Mall Gazette*

'Where there's a will, there are relations.'
    Michael Gill

'The spirit of adventure makes for happy lives.'
    Freya Stark

'Malvern is about 8 miles from Worcester "as the
cock crows".' From A. C. Benson's *Diaries*

'True equality exists in the treatment of unequal things
unequally.' Aristotle

'Good temper is one of the great preservers
of the features.'
  James Northcote recorded by William Hazlitt

Dumas put on woollen socks whenever he had a love
scene to write.

'He came away from the meeting with his tail
between his teeth.'
  Overheard by Jock Murray

'It is chance that makes brothers, but hearts that make
friends.' Von Geibel

A delegate at a Brighton Conservative Party conference
said that steel was being made into a political football.

'Laugh and the world laughs with you. Snore and you
sleep alone.'
  Anthony Burgess

'The rat historian' *Daily Telegraph* misprint when
referring to Sir Anthony Blunt

'The chains of habit are too weak to be felt until they are
too strong to be broken.' Dr Johnson

'Equality of opportunity means equal opportunity
to be unequal.'
  Iain Macleod, quoted by Lord Boyd Carpenter
  in *Way of Life*

The *Cornhill Magazine* cover by W. J. Linton
as it was when John Murray took over Smith Elder,
its original publisher

Word breaks:

Mans-
laughter

not-
iced

the-
rapist

to-
wed

ex-
porter

the leg-
end of King Arthur's table

gene-
ration

one of the male-
factors

no-
table

'It is a secret in the Oxford sense. You may tell it to only one person at a time.' Lord Franks

'A statesman, it is said, is a man who is thinking of the next generation – a politician is one who is thinking of the next election.'
   John Glubb reviewing the King of Jordan's memoirs

'Marriage is a chain so heavy that it always takes two people to carry it – sometimes three.'

'The great object of life is sensation – to feel that we exist.' Byron

'One of my sorrows is that I have no chit-chat to put out in a drawing-room.' Lord Wavell to Freya Stark

'Psychiatry is the disease of which it claims to be the cure.'

'The art of hospitality is to make guests feel at home when you wish they were.'

Aphra Behn's tombstone in Westminster Abbey composed by her lover:

> 'Here lies proof that wit can never be
> Defence against mortality.'

'I don't know about getting married – after all one might be left a widow.' Mabel Bradbury to her sister Dorothy

'It is being said that the supporters of the new grouping
lack weight in depth.' On a Labour Party split

Kenneth Clark's secretary to Jock Murray: 'Oh
Mr Murray, can Lord Clark ring you back as he's
at present tied up in the bathroom?'

'Liberty is more important than equality, with which
it is incompatible.' Raymond Mortimer

'It requires in these times much more intellect to
marshal so much greater a stock of ideas and
observations . . . hence the multitude of thoughts only
breeds increase of uncertainty. Those who should be
guides of the rest, see too many sides to every question.
They hear so much said and find that so much can be
said about everything that they feel no assurance about
the truth of anything.'
   John Stuart Mill in his diary on the doubts of the
   middle class

'They were equal because they were complementary.'
   Laurence Brande, *Four Acres of our Own*

'To the young – beware of imagination.
To be led by it is to follow a rainbow.
Beware of indecision, it neutralizes every virtue.'
   Lady Anne Barnard

'Work is the grand cure of all the maladies that ever
test mankind.' Thomas Carlyle

36

For Jock with many thanks from.

Osbert, who is not working nearly as hard here— as he was made to at

DAILY EXPRESS

MR. MURRAY
N.B.

1961

On occasion Jock brought down the portcullis at
No. 50 to prevent Osbert Lancaster from escaping
to the Garrick Club before completing the
introduction to a new collection of his Pocket
Cartoons – hence his comparison between pressure
of work at the *Daily Express* and at No. 50

At a meeting in Dover of ferry companies opposed to the Channel Tunnel, a P&O executive, Frank Oldham, declared: 'A lot of water has to pass under the bridge before the Channel Tunnel can get off the ground.'

In Blairgowrie Jock asked a Scot in the road where he could find a bookshop: 'Och but we're ne'er so up in the world for a thing like that.'

A journalist from a smart American magazine interviewing Elizabeth Longford: 'And in your long married life, Lady Longford, have you ever contemplated divorce?' Elizabeth Longford: 'Murder often, divorce never.'

'I deny nothing but doubt everything.' Byron

'She that is loved is safe and he that loves joyful.'
   From a Jeremy Taylor sermon

'Woman was made after man, and man has been after her ever since.'

'Many a man has a bonfire in his heart and nobody comes to warm himself at it. The passers-by notice only a little smoke coming from the chimney and go away.'
   Van Gogh

'The head cannot take in more than the seat can endure.'
   Winston Churchill on long speeches

An American newspaper reported that a couple married
for 65 years were applying for a divorce. The magistrate
asked why they had not divorced sooner: 'We felt we
ought to wait until the children were dead.'

'Tomorrow is my birthday, I shall have completed 30 and
3 years . . . and I go to bed with a heavy heart at having
lived so long.' Byron in 1821

'There is nothing like getting a good lie off one's chest.'

'Comfort must not be expected by those who go
a-pleasuring.' Byron

'He made a most delible impression on me.'

'His heart was in the right place but he always put his
foot in it.'
  From Patrick Leigh Fermor

'Under certain circumstances profanity provides a relief
denied even to prayer.' Mark Twain

'I have a simple philosophy. Fill what's empty, empty
what's full, and scratch where it itches.'
  Alice Roosevelt Longworth

'Life is what happens while you are making other plans.'
  John Lennon

'There lives more faith in honest doubt.' Tennyson

'The only reason why some people get lost in thought is because it is unfamiliar territory.' Paul Fix

'Democracy substitutes election by the incompetent many for appointment by the corrupt few.'
  George Bernard Shaw

'To my deafness I'm accustomed,
To my dentures I'm resigned,
I can manage my bifocals,
But Oh how I miss my mind.'
  From Alec Douglas Home

'The principal task of civilization, its actual *raison d'être*, is to defend us against nature.'
  Sigmund Freud

'Christianity has done a great deal for love by making a sin of it.' Anatole France

'I'm afraid of going to church for fear of hearing something very extraordinary.' Lord Melbourne, recorded in Queen Victoria's *Journal*

'All this talk of art is dangerous, it brings the ears so forward that they act as blinkers.'
  Edwin Lutyens to Clough Williams-Ellis

'Beware of women – they always have a manuscript hidden about their person.'
  Logan Pearsall Smith in a letter to Hugh Trevor-Roper

Wood engraving for the *Cornhill Magazine*
by Eric Ravilious

'She wore her good looks as a weapon.'
  From Colin Thubron

'I fancy some meddlesome saint or other has made you ill to make your friends feel how much your friendship means to them. As the trick has succeeded terribly well in my case, please send your understudy to pray to St Meddlesome to drop it.'
  George Bernard Shaw to Dame Laurentia McLachlan
  of Stanbrook Abbey

'When as a child I laughed and wept
Time crept.
When as a youth I dreamt and talked
Time walked.
When I became a full-grown man
Time ran.
And later as older I grew
Time flew.
Soon shall I find when travelling on
Time gone.
Will Christ have saved my soul by then?
Amen.'

'The less one has to do, the less time one finds to do it.'

'No bird soars too high if he soars with his own wings.'
  William Blake

'"Am I boring you, Lord Hugh?" "Not yet," replied my uncle.' From David Cecil

'Good news seldom arrives in a buff envelope.'

'I'm really not much of a drinker,
Just 1 or 2 at the most,
With 3 I'm under the table,
With 4 I'm under my host.'
  Dorothy Parker

'You must come again when you have less time.'
  Walter Sickert to Denton Welch

'There is less to him than meets the eye.'
  Tallulah Bankhead

'As a general rule, philosophy is like stirring mud or not
letting sleeping dogs lie.' Samuel Butler

'Success reveals infirmities which failure would
otherwise conceal.'
  John Stuart Mill, *On Liberty*

'The future isn't what it used to be.'

'Never run after a street car, or a girl, because another
one will be along in a minute.' Old American saying sent
to Captain Henry Denham when in hospital aged 80
with his leg in plaster having fallen when running
to catch a number 19 bus in Piccadilly

'A man must carry knowledge with him if he would
bring home knowledge.' Dr Johnson

A doodle from Hugh Casson on being sent best
wishes by Jock on his retirement as President of
the Royal Academy of Arts

'Let us not take too much delight in pleasures we cannot long enjoy, nor grieve with too much dejection for evils which cannot long be felt.'
  Dr Johnson on his 75th birthday to Robert
  Chamber, 1783

'I have no room for new ideas.' Jonathan Swift in advanced old age

'One of the finest minds in Britain until he makes it up'
  Of Enoch Powell

'We act as though comfort and luxury were the chief requirements of life, when all we need to make us really happy is something to be enthusiastic about.'
  Charles Kingsley

'The wider our experience, the deeper our tolerance'
  On a calendar

'History is not what happened, it is what you can remember.' *1066 and All That*

> 'Preserve me from my calling's snare
> And hide my simple heart above,
> Above the thorns of choking care,
> The gilded baits of worldly love.'
> Charles Wesley, Hymn 69, *English Hymnal*

'Art begins with craft, and there is not art until craft has been mastered.' Anthony Burgess

'It is necessary to be pushing – but fatal to seem so.'
  Benjamin Jowett's rule

'Flattery is alright if you don't inhale.'
  Adlai Stevenson

'From the inability to let well alone; from too much zeal
for the new and contempt for what is old; from putting
knowledge before wisdom, science before art, and clever-
ness before common sense; from treating patients as
cases, and from making the cure of the disease more
grievous than its endurance, Good Lord deliver us.'
  Sir Robert Hutchinson, Physician

'Say what you have to say in the fewest possible words.'
  Sir Arthur Bryant

'News is what governments don't want the public to
know.' Donald Trelford

'Travel makes one modest.' Flaubert

'I have always maintained that whether a black cat
crossing your path is lucky or unlucky depends on
whether you are a man or a mouse.'
  Bernard Levin

'He has, thank goodness, a certain amount of original sin
in him. It reveals itself in rather quiet, pleasant ways. His
work has been very neat, and rather good.'
  Jock's report for maths at Eton, 1923

'Can grapes be picked from briars or figs from thistles?'
  Matthew, 7:16

'He tries to get off with women because he cannot
get on with them.'

Winston Churchill was once referred to as a pillar of the
Church. 'No, no,' he replied, 'not a pillar of the Church
but a buttress, supporting it from the outside.'

'The optimist proclaims that we live in the best of all
possible worlds; the pessimist fears this is true.'

Byron said that the only way of conquering cant (and
hypocrisy) was ridicule – 'the only weapon that the
English climate cannot rust'.

'The advantage of being married to an archaeologist is
that the older you get, the more interested he becomes in
you.' Agatha Christie

'The thought of him [William Morris] has always
slightly irritated me. Of course he was a wonderfully
all-round man, but the act of walking round him has
always tired me.'
  Max Beerbohm to Sam Behrman

'If you know nothing about people, you can believe
anything about them.'
  Dervla Murphy in *Tales from Two Cities* referring to
  racial minorities in inner cities

47

JOHN MURRAY

JOHN MURRAY

Some of Jock's favourite designs for borders together with
Reynolds Stone's JOHN MURRAY

'If I esteemed you less, Envy would kill.'
  From Shelley's sonnet on Byron

The Irish definition of a queer: 'A man who prefers
women to drink.'

'A retrospective shudder.' Nietzsche's phrase for
remembering a near disaster

'A black social worker has been suspended from
duty by the left-wing Southwark Council for
calling her Asian boss a coconut.'
  Evening Standard , 1987

Publisher to author: 'It is a remarkable write, but
not an irresistible read.'

'They are agreeable enough but if they'd been books I
shouldn't have read them.'
  Young Goethe to his mother about fellow guests

'All the characters in this book are entirely
fictitious, and any person claiming to be any
one of them will be prosecuted.'
  Author's note in a book

'Toleration is a necessary consequence of our being
human. We are all products of frailty — fallible and prone
to error — so let us mutually pardon each other's follies.
This is . . . the first principle of all human rights.'
  Voltaire

'One has to resign oneself to being a nuisance if one
wants to get anything done.'
  Freya Stark

'It is almost a definition of a gentleman that he never
inflicts pain.' Cardinal Newman

'Man is not old when his hair turns grey,
Man is not old when his teeth decay,
But man is approaching his long last sleep
When his mind makes appointments his body
cannot keep.'
  From Jock's physiotherapist

Charles Dickens's philosophy of life: 'Action, usefulness
... the determination to be of service – we must all
be up and doing something.'
  From Paul Johnson's review of *Dickens's Letters*

'Curiosity is one thing invincible in nature.'
  Freya Stark

'Congratulations on having the only non-malignant part
of you removed.'
    Evelyn Waugh to Randolph Churchill who had gone
    into hospital for the removal of a growth which turned
    out to be benign

'If you have nothing good to say about anyone,
come and sit by me.'
  Alice Roosevelt Longworth

'To those who believe in God, no explanation is necessary.
To those who do not, no explanation is possible.'

'As I don't expect much, I can never be much
disappointed.' John Gay

'It is easy to be solemn, it is so hard to be frivolous.'
  G. K. Chesterton

'We trained hard; but it seems that every time we were
beginning to form into a team we would be reorganized.
I was to learn later in life that we tend to meet any new
situation by reorganizing, and a wonderful method it can
be for creating the illusion of progress while producing
confusion, inefficiency and demoralization.'
  Titus Petronius

'We must respect the living but the truth is good enough
for the dead.' Voltaire on biography

'The question with me is not whether you have the
right to render your people miserable, but whether
it is in your interest to make them happy.'
  Edmund Burke

'Expect the worst,
hope for the best,
and take what comes.'

'You never know what health is till you lose it.'
  An Indian sage

'No mind is thoroughly well organized that is
deficient in a sense of humour.'
  Samuel Taylor Coleridge

'The English are not happy unless they are miserable,
The Irish are not at peace unless they are at war,
The Scots are not at home unless they are abroad.'
  George Orwell

Voltaire on his deathbed was advised to renounce the
devil. He replied: 'Now is not the time to make enemies.'

'Remember when you go out with gentlemen never to
take wine. It's exciting enough without.'
  Dame Alix Meynell's grandmother to her mother

'At the back of every great fortune lies a great crime.'
  Balzac

Someone said to Heinrich Heine on his deathbed:
'Dieu vous pardonnera.' Heine replied, 'Oui, c'est
son métier.'

'Most of my friends seem to be either dead, extremely
deaf or living on the wrong side of Kent.'
  John Gielgud

'Old age is not for sissies.' From Janet Adam Smith

'A red herring that won't hold water'
  From a speech in the House of Lords

The MSS text in the illustration reads:

M.S.S
To JOHN MURRAY
50 ALBEMARLE ST.
LONDON ENGLAND

An intrepid Murray travel writer on her way to deliver
her typescript to 50 Albemarle Street.
Osbert Lancaster

'To make men socialists is nothing, but to make socialists human is a great thing.' Oscar Wilde

'Arguing with a woman is like trying to fold the airmail edition of *The Times* in a high wind.' Lord Mancroft

'If you are tired of sin, come in. If not ring . . . '
    Notice pinned to the outside of a Liverpool church

'Beware of loose women in tight skirts and tight women in loose skirts.'

Cardinal Manning's only indulgence was to sit in front of an open fire watching the tongues of flame which he said were the only tongues that did not speak and told no lies.

'Thrift is what you do to yourself; meanness is what you do to others.'

'Who breathes must suffer,
Who thinks must mourn,
And he alone is blest
who ne'er was born.'
    A note left with child No. 734 by its mother at
    Coram's Foundling Hospital in the 18th century

'People say life is the thing, but I prefer reading.'
    Logan Pearsall Smith

'It appears always easier to recognize inhumanity when it lies on someone else's doorstep.' Mahatma Gandhi

'Nothing ever becomes real until it is experienced.'
  Keats

'Critics are to authors what dogs are to lamp-posts.'
  Jeffrey Robinson

'Freedom of speech becomes less of a freedom if one is compelled to listen.'
  Mark Rogers of Jones and Evans Bookshop, Queen Victoria Street

'Life is a sexually transmitted disease.'
  The Faber Book of Fevers

'Whenever I feel the need for exercise I go and lie down for half an hour until the feeling passes.' Will Rogers

'He has no more patients because his patients are no more.' Byron on Dr Polidori

'It is possible to be born an aristocrat without ever becoming a gentleman.'
  Nicholas Ridley's comments on Germans and Italians from *Le Monde*

'Experience should tell us that secrecy is the handmaiden to bad government.' Peter Kellner, *The Independent*

'God preserve me from the man I trust. From the one I mistrust I can defend myself.' Written on the wall of a prison by a prisoner about to be executed

Some of Jock's favourite rules used in many of his books

'To be ignorant of what occurred before you were born is to remain a child forever.' Cicero

'There is always something rather ridiculous about the past.' Max Beerbohm

Lord Chesterfield on sex: 'The expense is damnable, the pleasure momentary and the position ludicrous.'

'You have the opportunity of moulding the future of the meat trade to make it shine like a beacon through the ages. It will be your finest hour.'
In a speech at the conference of the National Federation of Meat Traders, 1945

'The best thing about travel is that it teaches what are the places that are not worth seeing.'
Pierre Bénoit

'The good are so harsh to the clever, the clever so rude to the good.' Miss Wordsworth

'I hope I may die before you, so that I may see Heaven before you improve it.'
A remark made to Capability Brown

The danger of misplaced punctuation can be disastrous: 'You must never think you are in this world solely for the purpose of making money,' became in a report of a bishop's sermon, 'You must never think. You are in this world solely for the purpose of making money.'

'There is a middle state between love and friendship more delightful than either but more difficult to remain in.' Walter Savage Landor

'How do I know what I think till I hear what I say?'
  From Peter Quennell

'Far more people were sung into heresy than argued into it.' In *Hymns and the Reformation*

'Personal responsibility increases as that of the Gods decreases.'
  André Gide

'He that has a secret should not only hide it but hide that he has it to hide.'
  Thomas Carlyle

'If you destroy leisure, you destroy civilization.'
  John Kenneth Galbraith

'This is at heart rather a sensible and sober piece of work if you are able to cut through the first 200 or so pages to the epilogue.'
  From a review of *Apocalypse*

'To be uncertain is uncomfortable; but to be certain is ridiculous.' Goethe

'When words lose their meaning, people lose their freedom.' Confucius

Arthur Rackham's frontispiece for
Walter Starkie's *Don Gypsy*

'The centipede was happy quite
Until a frog for fun,
Said "Pray which leg goes after which?"
This brought her mind to such a pitch
She lay distracted in a ditch
Considering how to run.'

'You can lead a whore to culture but you cannot
make her think.'
   Dorothy Parker on being challenged to frame a
   sentence including the word 'horticulture'

On hearing the news that President Calvin Coolidge had
died, Dorothy Parker exclaimed: 'How could they tell?'

From Stewart Perowne, 1956
   Four rules of politics in the Middle East:
      1. Always keep the initiative
      2. Always exploit the inevitable
      3. Always keep in with the 'outs'
      4. Never stand between a dog and a lamp-post

'Silence, it has been said, is a virtue which renders us
agreeable to our fellow creatures.'

'There is no possible doubt that one thing leads to
another.' From Margaret Lane

'It is rarely possible to carry the torch of truth through a
crowd without singeing somebody's beard.'
   Joshua Bruyn

'A little turmoil, now and then, is an agreeable quickener
of the sensations.' Byron

'Nobody is despised by other people unless he has
first lost his respect for himself.' Seneca

What is the difference between the various political
systems? H. Williams' Chairman, John J. Quin, gave
his shareholders the following answer:
> 'Socialism is when you have two cows and give
> one to your neighbour.
> Communism is when you have two cows and the
> state takes both and gives you milk.
> Fascism is when you have two cows and the state
> takes both and sells you milk.
> Nazism is when you have two cows and the state
> takes both and shoots you.
> Capitalism is when you have two cows, sell one and
> buy a bull.
> Bureaucracy is when you have two cows and the
> state takes both, shoots one, milks the other
> and pours the milk down the drain.'

In 1945 Gulbenkian announced negotiations for the
reconstruction of the consortium known as the Iranian
Petroleum Company. 'We have succeeded', an Anglo-
Iranian executive said, 'in making the Agreement
completely unintelligible to anyone.' 'No one will ever
be able to litigate about these documents', said one of the
Gulbenkian lawyers, 'because no one will be able to
understand them.'

61

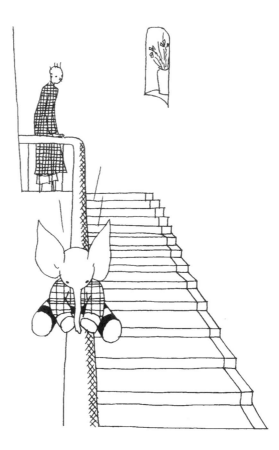

Mumfie the Elephant enjoying the quick way down the
stairs at 50 Albemarle Street watched by Scarecrow.
Katharine Tozer

Dr Johnson on divorce laws: 'Nature has given
women so much power that the law has very wisely
given them little.'

'Those who cannot remember the past are
condemned to repeat it.' Santayana

'Our two peoples have an infinite capacity for mutual
misunderstanding.'
  Dr Garrett Fitzgerald of the Irish and the English

'Please don't talk while I am interrupting.'
  Todd Rockefeller

Princess Margaret's lady-in-waiting opened a wedding
present for her: it turned out to be a wooden salad server.
Carved along its extended handle were the words: 'May
your Life be one long Spoon.'
  From Osbert Lancaster

'I feel like giving you the length of my tongue to inform
you that I want you to take me as one of your traders.'
  A letter received by John Murray from Ghana, 1958

'Nescit vox missa reverti.' – 'The word once uttered
returns not.' *The Epistle of Paul to the Hebrews*

'Worcester, like most colleges, does not admit dogs.
The Dean's dog Flint has thus been officially
declared a cat by the Governing Body.'
  From the Oxford magazine *Isis*

'The common fate of the indolent is to see their rights become the prey of the active. The condition upon which God hath granted liberty to mankind is eternal vigilance.' John Philpott Curran

Bishop Jeremy Taylor on the state of marriage: 'It hath in it less of beauty but more of safety than the single life; it hath more care, but less danger; it is more merry, and more sad; it is fuller of sorrows, and fuller of joys; it lies under more burdens, but is supported by all the strengths of love and charity, and these burdens are delightful.'

'Moisture in tobacco, Mr Speaker, is one of those thorny subjects which has long been a bone of contention.'
        C. T. Ritchie when Chancellor of the Exchequer in the House of Commons, *circa* 1902

'We cannot discuss afforestation in a watertight compartment.'
        From a speech in the House of Commons

'Those who carry on great public schemes must be proof against the worst delays, the most mortifying disappointments, the most shocking of insults and, what is worst of all, the presumptuous judgements of the ignorant upon their designs.'
        Edmund Burke

'Those who rest on their laurels find themselves sitting on a thorn bush.'

64

Lockington Church, Leicestershire, visited
by Jock with John Betjeman and John Piper.
John Piper

'Sir, I have been commissioned by Michael Joseph to
write an autobiography and I would be grateful to any
of your readers who could tell me what I was doing
between 1960 and 1974.'
    A letter from Jeffrey Bernard in the *New Statesman*,
    18 July 1975

One doctor to another:
'About the termination of pregnancy – I want
your opinion. The father was syphilitic. The mother
tuberculous. Of the children born the first was
blind, the second died, the third was deaf and dumb,
the fourth was tuberculous. What would you have done?'
  'I would have ended the next pregnancy.'
  'Then you would have murdered Beethoven.'
    Maurice Baring

'A house unkept cannot be so distressing as a life
unlived.' From one of Rose Macaulay's novels

Advice given by a doctor to people with eating neuroses:
'Eat what kind nature doth bestow
It will amalgamate below
If the mind says it shall be so.
But once the mind begins to doubt
Your gastric juice will find you out.'

A mother whale's advice to her young: 'Beware, my
dears, it is when you are spouting that you are most
likely to be harpooned.'
    A useful opening to a speech when excusing its brevity

John Piper recording architectural details in
preparation for the Murray Architectural Guides which
he wrote with John Betjeman.
Osbert Lancaster

The arrival of a bestseller at 50 Albemarle Street
together with its intrepid author.

Osbert Lancaster

PROVERBS

A Christmas card to Jock and Diana
from John Craxton

'You cannot stop the birds of sorrow from flying over your head but you can prevent them from building nests in your beard.' Chinese

'Better a wise enemy than a foolish friend.' Turkish

'The diver who thinks on the jaws of a crocodile will never gather pearls.'

'If you want to be happy for a day, get drunk. If you want to be happy for a week, get married. If you want to be happy for life, become a gardener.' Chinese

'Take opportunity by the forelock, for it has a bald behind.' Persian

'Peace is the result of understanding, not of an agreement.' Arab

'Any plan is bad which is not susceptible to change.' Italian

'Even a beetle is a beauty in the eyes of its mother.'

'God gives nuts to those who have no teeth.'

'He who sees a need and waits to be asked for help is as unkind as if he had refused it.' Dante

'Vagueness is often a virtue.' Japanese

'A god lives in a cloud.' Japanese

'There is a time to wink as well as see.'

'Honey is sweet but the bee stings.'

'Glasses and lasses are brittle ware.'

'Love is blind but marriage restores the sight.'

'Truth cannot be put on one's fingertip.'
  Japanese

'The truest wealth is that of understanding.'

'The wise man has long ears, big eyes and a short
tongue.'   Russian

'The rogue believes every man to be of his own stamp.'
  Spanish

'Better the cold blast of winter than the hot breath of
a pursuing elephant.'

'A falsehood mixed with expediency is better than
a truth that stirs trouble.' The Persian poet Sa'adi

'Wit is the salt of conversation, not the food.'
  William Hazlitt

'Hear twice before you speak once.'

'High regions are never without storms.'

'I thought myself badly off because I had no boots, until
I went out and met a man who had no legs.' Chinese

'Every bleat loses a mouthful.' Chinese

'A narrow mind has a broad tongue.' Arab

'It is better to do a kind deed on your own doorstep than
to travel 1,000 miles to burn incense.' Chinese

'To hear is to forget,
to read is to learn,
to do is to know.' Chinese

'One and one make eleven.' Oriental

'God makes a man lose his donkey so that he can give
him the pleasure of finding it again.' Turkish

'The eye of the master fattens the horse.' Arab

'If you are to be hung, you'd better be hung by
an English rope.' Turkish saying

'There is no spectacle more agreeable than to
observe an old friend fall from a rooftop.'
  Kai Lung

'One tongue is enough for two women.'

73

Orlando sends Greetings
to all his
Friends.
(He died, aged 19½, November 5ᵗʰ.)

On the death of Orlando the Marmalade Cat,
Kathleen Hale sent Jock this picture of his
new life in heaven

'It is a false economy to burn your house down out of a desire to inconvenience your mother-in-law.'

'You can't have a full barrel and a drunk wife.'

'For a marriage to be peaceful the husband should be deaf and the wife blind.' Spanish

'He who speaks last, wins.' Spanish

'Life is a mirror: if you frown at it, it frowns back; if you smile, it returns the greeting.' Thackeray

'A kiss that speaks volumes is rarely a first edition.'
  From a Christmas cracker

'The empty vessel makes the greatest sound.'
  Shakespeare

'A fool throws a stone into the sea and a hundred wise men cannot pull it out.'
  Cypriot

'All men are of the same mould, but some are mouldier than others.'

'It is good to know the truth and speak it, but it is better to talk of palm trees.' Chinese

'The couple who go to bed only to save candles may end up with twins.' Chinese

'Among wolves, howl like a wolf.' Russian

'True faith sees an oasis when it looks at the desert.'
   Turkish

'Believe your own eyes rather than others' mouths.'
   Turkish

'Work is often the father of pleasure.' Voltaire

'Our senses don't deceive us: our judgement does.'
   Goethe

'Do not believe all you hear and do not tell all you see.'
   Turkish

'The fool looks in the mirror, the wise man sees himself
in the faces of his friends.' Chinese

'In the palace of delights there are no clocks.' Florentine

'If the counsel is good, no matter who gave it.'

'If you cannot bite, never show your teeth.'

'Do not remove a fly from your friend's head with a
hatchet.' Chinese

'The seeking for one thing will find another.' Irish

'You cannot eat a bun from the middle.' Hausa

76

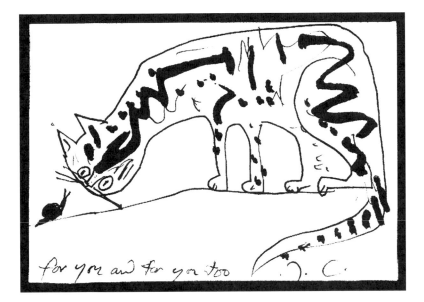

for you and for you too   J. C.

A Christmas card to Jock and Diana
from John Craxton

Workman's tea-break during the rebuilding of
the front wall of 50 Albemarle Street

DELIGHTFUL ODDITIES

The nuns of Stanbrook Abbey preparing to
empty their fishpond in search of a lost ring.
Sent to Jock after he mentioned to Val Biro
his visit to the nuns and their plight

What the brassière said to the top hat: 'You go on ahead while I give these two a lift.' Told to the ambassador in Cairo in 1942 by Freya Stark. It shocked him.

'Sex has become a serious international problem for which a solution hasn't yet been found.'
  Introduction to a TS *The Truth about Sex* submitted by A. M. Macrae, 1968

'The girl was beheaded, chopped into pieces and placed in a trunk but was not interfered with.'
  From a Fleet Street report

'What has one wheel and flies?'
'A wheelbarrow full of manure.'
  A riddle from John Piper

'What is funny about legs?'
'The bottom is at the top.'
  A riddle from a lady of 92

'I'm afraid', said a woman on entering a shoe shop, 'that one of my feet is larger than the other.' 'Oh no, madam,' exclaimed the salesman, 'if anything one is smaller.'

'Exclusive universal Tailors.' Advertisement

'Sole joint agents.' Sign outside a house

'Bric-à-brac bought / Antiques sold.'
  A notice inside a West Country shop

'Tattooed lady wishes to meet gentleman with similar views.' Advertisement from the agony column of the *Observer*

Notice in a Cork jeweller's window: 'Ears pierced while you wait.' From Dervla Murphy

Order from the Middle East for 2 copies of 'Riding on a Tigress' and 1 copy of 'The Cost of Incest' by Freya Stark (correct titles = *Riding to the Tigris* and *The Coast of Incense)*

'St Margaret's School of the Immaculate Conception for Girls', and underneath, 'Preparatory for Boys'
  Sign outside a school in Berkshire

Book on typewriting in 2 volumes:
 1. Direct Vertical Method
 2. Horizontal All Fingers Method

Gotobed, Allday and Knight. Solicitors in the City

Riddle from Anne Ridler:
Q. 'What is the difference between a snowman and a snow woman?'
A. 'Snowballs.'

'What is the difference between King David's third wife and a Cambridge female undergraduate?' 'One was Abishag, a Shunamite, the other shabby hag, the Newnhamite.'

Archibald - shielding Jumbo's
eyes from the sight of my
book.

Archibald Ormsby-Gore shielding Jumbo's eyes from
the sight of the more saucy pictures in *The Works*.
Beryl Cook sent this to Jock after reading
John Betjeman's *Archie and the Strict Baptists*

A warden in the dark outside an air-raid shelter during the war asked, 'Are there any pregnant mothers here?' A young cockney shouted, 'Give us a chance, guv', we've only been 'ere ten minutes.'

Notice seen in a butcher's shop in Westmorland: 'John Murray, seller of tripe'

'Little Marlow cemetery - no through road'
  Road sign on the approach to Marlow, Bucks

Hotel notice: 'If requiring breakfast please hang on door knob before 7 a.m.'

An old-time printer had his own quaint rule of punctuation. 'I set type as long as I can hold my breath,' he explained, 'and then I put in a comma. When I yawn I put in a semicolon. And when I want a chew of tobacco I make a paragraph . . . '

George Lichtenberg believed he wrote better poetry if he placed a camomile poultice behind his left ear.

A sign saying 'Harwich for the Continent' – and in chalk underneath – ' Frinton for the incontinent'

A doctor gave a patient who was a labourer two suppositories as part of a cure. When the patient came for his next appointment the doctor asked how things were progressing. 'For all the good they did I might as well have put 'em up my arse.'

'The lithography is finished,
likewise the lithographer.'
Kathleen Hale on completing *Orlando's Evening Out*

'Due to staff shortage the automatic ticket machines
are not in use.'
   Notice at Farringdon Underground station

Inland Revenue letter of October 1988: 'In spite of
continuing heavy arrears of work in this Division we will
award this correspondence a sizeable measure of priority.'
   About John Betjeman's copyright valuation

Wording on a form sent out by a Government
department in 1962: 'Separate departments on the
same premises are treated as separate premises for
this purpose where separate branches of work which
are commonly carried on as separate businesses in
separate premises are carried on in separate departments
of the same premises.'

'BATHS may be had (by arrangement) with the
manageress only.' Notice in a Southport hotel

Two palindromes from Bevis Hillier:

T. ELIOT, TOP BARD, NOTES PUTRID TANG
EMANATING, IS SAD. I'D ASSIGN IT A NAME -
GNAT DIRT UPSET ON DRAB POT TOILET
and
NOW STOP, MAJOR-GENERAL, ARE NEGRO
JAM-POTS WON

'Horse manure bagged 25p. Do it yourself 10p.'
   Advertisement outside a Sussex farm

'The reason why we can sell our antiques for less is
because we buy them direct from the manufacturer.'
   Advertisement in the *Washington Star*

'Emergency WC 20 miles.' Unhelpful sign on
the M40 just east of the Oxford turn-off

George Burney was asked at the age of 93 what sex was
like. He replied 'like playing billiards with a rope'.

Order from Websters Bookshop in Swaziland:
1 copy of 'In Ethiopia with a Male' by Dervla Murphy
(correct title = *In Ethiopia with a Mule*)

'Distance makes the hair grow longer.'
   Notice in a barber's shop window in Scotland

'King David and King Solomon
Led merry, merry lives
With lots and lots of concubines
And lots and lots of wives.
But when old age came o'er them
With many, many qualms,
King Solomon wrote the proverbs
And King David wrote the psalms.'

'He never used the things himself
He kept them glaring on the shelf,
And champing on the shelf beneath,
Were 27 sets of teeth.'
   On a collector of glass eyes

87

Signs seen on travels abroad

To move the cabin, push button for wishing floor. If the cabin should enter more persons, each one should press number of wishing floor. Driving is then going alphabetically by natural order.'
  In a Belgrade hotel lift

'French widows in every bedroom.'
  Advertisement in an Italian hotel

'You are invited to take advantage of the chambermaid.'
  In a Japanese hotel

In the lobby of a Moscow hotel across from a Russian Orthodox monastery: 'You are welcome to visit the cemetery where famous Russian and Soviet composers, artists, and writers are buried daily except Thursday.'

'Our wines leave you nothing to hope for.'
  On the menu of a Swiss restaurant

'For your convenience we recommend courteous, efficient self-service.'
  In a Hong Kong supermarket

'Salad a firm's own make; limpid red beet soup with cheesy dumplings in the form of fingers; roast duck let loose; beef rashers beaten in the country people's fashion' On the menu of a Polish hotel

'Well led hotel with comfort of nowadays and hot and
cold water running through all the bedrooms.'
  Bavarian hotel notice

'If you must smoke in bed please inform the
Management where you wish your ashes sent.'
  Notice in bedrooms in a New York hotel

'These little sisters solicit gentle alms, they do not
respect religion and harbour all manner of disease.'
  A notice outside an Italian hospital run by nuns

'Please do not throw cigarette ends down the lavatory. It
makes them soggy and very difficult to light.'
  Notice in a restaurant in Rome

Inspired by Lesley Blanch's *The Wilder Shores of Love*,
Maudie Littlehampton sets out.
Osbert Lancaster

EMBLEMS OF
CHRISTIAN LIFE

Jock was fascinated by the seven deadly sins and although he did not lose sight of the cardinal virtues, they never offered the same appeal to him. He was also delighted to have played a part, while on the Archbishop of Canterbury's copyright committee, in saving 'the devil and all his works' from being rendered 'politically unacceptable' in the revision of the Prayer Book. Perhaps this is why there is a predominance of emblems relating to man's weaknesses in this book — their macabre nature particularly intrigued him.

A number of these designs (taken from *Emblems of Christian Life* illustrated by W. Harry Rogers, Griffith Farran, London) were used in books which Jock published, such as John Betjeman's *First and Last Loves*. He also used some on compliments slips for special occasions. I often wondered whether the recipients fully grasped the messages they conveyed.

They shall beat their swords into plowshares, and their spears into pruning-hooks : nation shall not lift up sword against nation, neither shall they learn war any more.

Isaiah, ii. 4.

PEACE

A good foundation against the time to come, that they may lay hold on eternal life.

1 Timothy, vi. 19.

UNITY

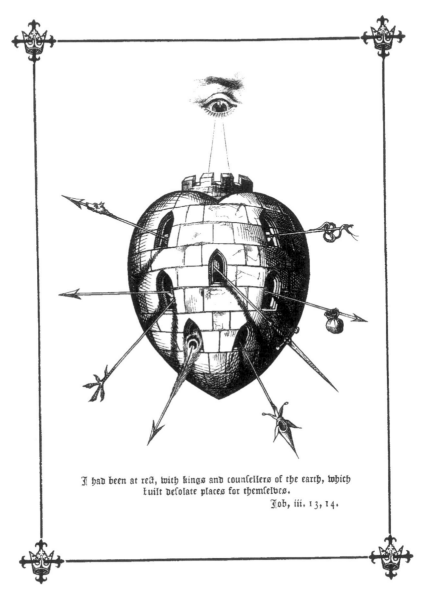

I had been at rest, with kings and counsellers of the earth, which built desolate places for themselves.

Job, iii. 13, 14.

SOLITUDE

How shall we sing the Lord's song in a strange land?
Ps. cxxxvii. 4.

CAPTIVITY

For the wicked boasteth of his heart's desire, and blesseth the covetous, whom the Lord abhorreth.

Psalms, x. 3.

INDULGENCE

If I have walked with vanity, or if my foot hath hasted to deceit.

Job, xxxi. 5.

GREED

He hath set the world in their heart.
Eccles. iii. 11.

WORLDLINESS

Ye also outwardly appear righteous unto men, but within ye are
full of hypocrisy and iniquity.

Matt. xxiii. 28.

HYPOCRISY

They that sow in tears shall reap in joy.

Ps. cxxvi. 5.

BITTER SWEET

They shall hunt them from every mountain, and from every hill, and out of the holes of the rocks. Jer. xvi. 16.

VENGEANCE

Which will not hearken to the voice of charmers, charming never so wisely.

Ps. lviii. 5.

TEMPTATION

Wrath killeth the foolish man.
Job, v. 2.

Cease from anger, and forsake wrath.
Ps. xxxvii. 8.

ANGER

To Jock and Diana with love from Paddy

12. 9. 77

A characteristic inscription by Paddy Leigh Fermor
in *A Time of Gifts*

ACKNOWLEDGEMENTS

I would like to offer special thanks to all those who have
so kindly given support and valuable criticism during the
gestation of this volume. It has been great fun trying to
establish attributions – some sayings have been attrib-
uted to as many as four people – but with expert advice
these have usually been reduced to one (sometimes the
most likely of several where there is no documentary
evidence).

As to the illustrations and decorations, these are a
major part of the book and I am particularly grateful
to all those who created them, or in their absence to the
copyright owners (where these could be traced), for so
generously allowing them to be reproduced. In all cases
permission was given freely as a tribute to my father.

All royalties from the sale of this book will be used for
the restoration of the John Murray historical ledgers and
letter books so that they can be safely handled by
researchers in the future.

John R. Murray

by John Bratby

by Derek Hill

by John Springs

by Freya Stark

Four portraits of Jock

PERSONAL ADDITIONS

The following pages have been
left blank so that readers can add
their own favourites, thus giving
the book continuing life.

John Craxton